Precarius

GOD WANTS TO HEAR FROM YOU

Kimberly E.M. Beasley

HunnyChild Books

Unless otherwise indicated, all Scripture quotations are from the Holy Bible, English Standard Version® (ESV®) Copyright © 2001 by Crossway, a publishing ministry of Good News Publishers. Used by permission. All rights reserved.

"The Constitution of the United States," Preamble

Copyright © 2015 Kimberly E.M. Beasley

All rights reserved.

ISBN: 0990948234
ISBN-13: 978-0-9909482-3-0

DEDICATION

This book is dedicated to Carlotta, my angel! You taught me to say my name with pride and confidence. You made me pray even when I didn't want to. You are an angel and my encounter with you changed the course of my life.

CONTENTS

Acknowledgments

Preface

	Introduction	5
1	What Is Prayer?	9
2	Who Should Pray and To Whom?	15
3	When Should We Pray?	23
4	Where Should We Pray?	29
5	Why Should We Pray?	37
6	How Should We Pray?	43
7	Prayers of David	47
8	Prayer Journaling 36.5 Days of Prayer	59
	About the Author	101

ACKNOWLEDGMENTS

Lord above all, I thank you!

To my parents and memory of my grandparents. Thank you for teaching me the importance of prayer and not just going to church but developing a personal relationship with God. The greatest message you have ever given me is branded in my soul…"Prayer changes things!"

To my Great Aunts: Anna, May and Ethel Mae. "Don't worry about me I got JC, My Daddy, My Mommy…Don't worry about me." I love you all dearly!

To everyone that has ever uttered sacred words of prayer for me. I am grateful for you and pray that God will not withhold any good thing from you. Thank you! Your prayers fortified my resolve and were not in vain.

To Mary Stephens; In 1998 I told you I was going to write a book and would acknowledge you. I'm keeping my word. Thank you for believing in me.

PREFACE

There is nothing more common and complex among people; no other practice more mysterious and misconstrued than prayer. The ancient art of prayer has been practiced in seemingly every culture, on every continent throughout all civilizations. Of course there are skeptics and antagonists who believe that praying by no means impact human experience or the course of life. It's merely human delusion and a fanatical religious ritual.

As children we are taught to say certain prayers but never thoroughly explained why. We merely repeat what our parents tell us, commit it to memory and recite them each time we're told to say our prayers. We were told there was a god listening but we couldn't see him. How foolish is it to believe that there is someone out there listening to our complaints, concerns and requests? Is prayer really a human invention designed as an outlet for human fears, frustrations, and anxiety? Is it nothing more than a psychological experience that eases the mind and help people cope with life's challenges? So what if it is? What's wrong with that? But what if it's not an illusion and you find that prayer really does impact the human experience and the course of life; will you pray then?

It seems the human spirit is naturally drawn to this invisible and mysterious entity for some reason unbeknownst to us; even with all the questions that arise regarding it. I know I have had questions regarding prayer and have even tried avoiding it many times. At times I was afraid to ask questions about it. I even did it without believing or knowing why I was doing it. It was simply ritualistic and redundant. It seemed fruitless, powerless, and pointless. I was suffering from a quiet disillusionment with my experience with prayer.

Despite all the questions and ambiguity surrounding prayer, it is still one of the most communal practices we have today. Many biblical characters and historical figures had profound committed lives of prayer. Among those were Ramses, Moses, Abraham, David, Solomon, Jesus, Prophet Muhammad, Harriet Tubman, Frederick Douglas, Gandhi, Dr. Martin Luther King Jr., and John F Kennedy (pbut) to name a few. If you research some of the prayers they prayed, the impact prayer had on their lives and the lives of others is evident. This affirms one thing is certain: No matter what we question about prayer, it somehow works.

Many will still find themselves fixated on the queries regarding prayer and it is this challenge we will embrace as we explore the "Who, What, When, Where, Why and How" questions about prayer.

INTRODUCTION

Presidents do it, Prime Ministers do it, Kings and Queens do it. Whether Jewish, Muslim, or Christian; religious and non-religious people alike do it. Everyone does it in some form or another. Some are certain it works and fewer devote their entire lives to it. What is it? The common and yet so uncommon act of Prayer!

Prayer could be considered as a global legacy that has been habitually fostered from generation to generation. Contrary to popular belief prayer is not just a religious practice. Because prayer is universal among varied religions, it does provide a sense of neutrality among them. Some could agree that prayer is a requirement that adherents should perform daily in most religions;

however it's not a product solely for the religious sect.

We all desire to understand prayer and have a yearning to connect with the Divine. Believe it or not it's actually innate for us to pray. God created us to commune with Him and not only Him but with each other as well. Prayer is not only one the most common practices among cultures, it seems to be one of the most intimidating as well. Where does this intimidation come from? Can we rid ourselves from it? The answer is…Yes!

It's Sunday morning around 4:00 A.M. my husband and I head to the church for early Morning Prayer. As I span the sanctuary I notice but a handful of people present. I questioned myself, "Where is everybody?" We attended pray every service and each time less and less people were present. I remember a time when there were three people there. This was baffling. I tried to encourage others to come to prayer but to no avail people were still not coming out. Eventually I stopped going.

One of the greatest gifts humans were given was the ability to pray. If there is one thing I know for certain is that many of my prayers have been answered. I also know that no matter who you are, anyone can pray and God hears and answers us all.

Prayer has been one of the most misunderstood practices worldwide. With all our efforts to explain the simplicity of praying we've managed to complicate a relatively simple means of communication.

Prayer is the most natural and truest form of dialog we actually practice. It's as natural as breathing. We are subconsciously praying all day every day. There is a constant dialog going on within us. We're given answers and direction without any persuasion. We go on daily and function without analyzing and questioning every little thing. We end our day, wake up and do it all over again.

The problem comes in when we have to consciously pray and focus our attention on a particular thing. Because of what we resolved were failed attempts in the past, we hold strong to our reservations about praying. It's no different than any other day and coasting along. The only thing is we are conscious of the event so it is amplified rather than subtle. If we took the time to look around us we will see trouble is happening everywhere and it doesn't last always. Instead we choose to panic and create all these what if scenarios. What's more delusional, praying, which is simply asking for help through an event or conjuring up something that hasn't even happened? Either way there's inner thought and dialog, results will be impending.

You can make a difference and change the course of your life by effectively praying. Join me on this venture as we delve into some modest questions and answers about prayer. Take control; don't let inertia destroy your prayer life.

1
WHAT IS PRAYER?

You pray and cry, pray and cry; then say, "I'm waiting on God." …WAIT! You pray and cry, pray and cry then say, "I'm waiting on God." …WAIT! Have you ever thought this is insane? Albert Einstein said *"Doing the same thing over and over again and expecting different results is insanity."* If you are praying and not getting the desired results then there is something wrong with your method of praying. It's not prayer itself it's the way you're implementing it. All prayers receive an answer. It might not be the answer you desired nonetheless it gets answered. Unfortunately we have been instructed wrong when it comes to prayer and we must retrain our mind in order to understand this spiritual notion and how it pertains to us.

In order for you to effectively practice something you must first understand what it is that you are doing. So before we go any further let's define what prayer is. The word "Prayer" is based on the Latin word "Precarius" meaning "obtained by entreaty." According to Google, Prayer (n): *"A solemn request for help or an expression of thanks addressed to God or an object of worship."* Webster defines "Prayer" as *"A set order of words."* Biblically the word "Prayer" means *"to petition, beg, beseech, supplication, request."* Interesting, whether secular or biblical "Prayer" is synonymous, interchangeable!

What should I pray about?

Now that we have actually defined what prayer is, you might be wondering, "What should I pray about?" You can pray about any and everything. Nothing is off limits. If it has any importance to you and that is subject to change at any given time…pray about it. The beauty about prayer nothing is too small or too grand to pray about. God is open to hearing it all. You must believe this! There is an element of faith that goes hand in hand with prayer. NO DOUBT! Doubt and worry cancels faith and you will receive the negative as a result of your disbelief because you put more faith in the negative instead of the positive outcome you desired. Don't focus and concentrate on what you don't want to happen. The "What Ifs." Rather focus your attention on what you do want to happen and stay focused. In the nutshell if you are going to pray about something by all means be specific and believe wholeheartedly that you'll receive nothing but the best. If you feel you need more faith, which is conviction, ask God to give you more. Don't be double-minded, timid or indecisive. Be clear, specific, detailed and bold. Another thing don't let inertia take over, do something in the same direction you focused your prayer.

For instance, I desired to write a book. I have always written poetry but never did anything with it. My husband would oftentimes say to me that I needed to do something with my writing. Well guess what I did? I prayed about it and that was that. Although I kept writing poems over the years, I never did anything in the direction of putting a book together. Well in 2013 I was diagnosed with cancer and as I suffered through radiation treatment and complications with my Lupus, my life seemed to be falling apart. It was at this time when I started evaluating my heart's desire and that was to be a motivational speaker and an award winning author. Well in 2014 I really started focusing my attention on my desire. I blocked out everything that I was going through and I focused only on what was really important to me and that was completing my book. Truth be told I was preparing to die, but I didn't want to leave this life without accomplishing what I had always wanted to be and that was to be an award winning author and motivational speaker. At this very moment I just realized that you have to be that urgent about your life and destiny, because this day is really your last day. We must live as if today is all we have because tomorrows ground is not stable enough to build upon and too uncertain for plans. If it be God's will that we live then tomorrows plans will be made. I speak by experience not theology and from application not theory that the prayers I have prayed concerning my desires have all been answered. To date my book "Revelations of my Heart" won the 2015 Texas Association of Authors First Place for the Best Poetry/Spiritual Book Award. I have been the keynote speaker for more than one event. I have sat on a speaker's panel and I'm looking forward to whatever comes next. My life is in a chronic state and I'm not spending any more time on inertia. Life is terminal and none of us knows when our clock will expire. So become critical about your time because once it's redeemed there's no refunding it.

What is the purpose of praying?

You might have asked the question, "What's the purpose of praying?" As many others have asked. My answer is simple, if you want to build a relationship with someone you must communicate with them. Most people view intimacy as something only physical but intimacy has two layers, spiritual and then physical. Intimate relationships should only be between you and the individual you're sharing intimate relation with. No one else! In this case we're speaking of intimacy with God. In order for you to build reverential intimacy with God prayer is the key. Know that you will never know everything there is to know about God. He is to complex, vast, multidimensional; we will never know who He is completely. What we do know is that He is the Creator of all, He is Love, Life, Merciful, Just, Gracious and Eternal to name a few attributes. We hold fast to what we know and build upon that faith.

Our prayer life gives us a picture of the type of relationship we have or are developing with God; distant or close. So no matter what people say to try to encourage you to pray more, it's up to you to determine your relationship and whether or not you want to build a deeper one.

Not only is building a relationship with God a valid purpose for praying but in doing so you ultimately get to know you better as well. Yes, through prayer God will reveal to you who you are and what your purpose is. Most people think that there is only one purpose in life for them to fulfil but that's not so. We serve several purposes in life at different stages of our lives. That's called growth. Look at a tree. As a seedling it never asks "What's my purpose?" Once it's planted, it just grows until it dies and returns to the earth. And even then it still helps to facilitate the process of life by aiding in the growth and continued life of other plants and wildlife. A tree gives shade and shelter for many generations and is not confused as when to spout or shed leaves. God set that in order and He set an order to our lives as well. It's up to you to find out what that order is and present purpose. Don't let others dictate to you what your purpose is. People will tell you their perspective as to who they think you are and what your role is. Know the truth about who you are, your true character and ability; know yourself authentically.

In case you're not clear about the purpose of praying:
1. To know and to learn to trust God
2. To know and accept yourself authentically.

2

WHO SHOULD PRAY AND TO WHOM?

If we take a moment, look around, we don't have to look very far, there is irrefutable evidence that our world is in need of hope. We are perplexed on every hand. We are plagued by threats of losing our jobs and terrorized by the images of death that inundates all avenues of media. We are disillusioned, the human condition is grave. Our nation is divided, our communities are failing, our families are broken and our children are suffering. We are crying out in anguish…HELP!

Who should pray? We…the people.

Who should we pray to?

God is greater than our religions. He's too vast to fit completely into any book. He's not concerned about our differences; because He created us all. You ask who should you pray too; I say, to God the creator of all things in heaven and on earth. The Self-Existent One, the One God Eternal, Omniscient all-knowing and all seeing. Who's Omnipresent; everywhere at every time and anywhere at any time. The Omnipotent, all powerful, great, mighty and majestic God. The One God that brings rain and causes the seasons to change. The One that told the oceans and seas to roll back at the shore. The God that secretly knit you together in the sanctuary of your mother's womb.

No one knows who HE is completely; all we know is that HE IS! He is Love, He is Life, He is God. The One and Only Creator and Sustainer. That is who you pray to. The more you pray, the more He'll reveal to you who He is and His list of attributes will become tailored to fit you and your experiences with Him. You can then say you know Him to be thus and so. As for me, I know Him to be my Comforter and Teacher to name a few. But I know Him to be so much more.

For those of you who think God won't hear you because of your indoctrination, this is especially for you. God forgives; forgiveness is freedom and it is for everyone. Forgiveness is a gift not only from God but a gift you need to give to yourself. You might be feeling guilty from past mistakes and feel you deserve to be punished over and over again. That's not so. If God forgives what seems to be the unforgivable why can't you. You are worthy of forgiveness. Stop reliving your past. All you're doing is hindering your present and prolonging your suffering; and for what? To prove that you're apologetic? Once time is redeemed there are no refunds. What is lost is lost and what is gained is gained. You must live on. Don't fear being rejected by God. Just come to Him with a sincere and truthful heart, there is nothing you can hide from Him. Allow Him to help you. Give it a try. What do you have to lose? You pray alone, no one knows what you're praying about, it's personal and completely confidential. It's an intimate encounter between you and Him. No one else.

There was a time when shame kept me from praying. I fought every impulse to pray. Intentionally ignored it; because I was ashamed. I was severely depressed and suicidal. I had gone through a divorce right after giving birth to my son. I was in an abusive marriage and refused to subject my innocent baby to any further mistreatment. A year after my divorce was final, my Grandmother passed away. I had no idea I was already depressed as a result of a failed marriage. When my Grandmother passed I hadn't experienced death that close before so I didn't know what grief was. So I started drinking and smoking marijuana every day after work. To add to the pressure I had come out of remission from cervical cancer; and May of 1998 I had a hysterectomy at the age of 23. To add insult to injury, I was let go from my job because my comp time ran out. To sum it all up; I was an abused, divorced, grief stricken, drug using, surgically barren, fearful, unemployed single mother. After all of these events I would be lying if I said I believed God would answer any of my prayers. So I didn't pray. It took until December of 1998 for me to hit rock bottom and I was prepared to give up everything. I was suicidal; I was lost and totally consumed in my despair and all I could say was "Lord, Help Me!" as I laid on my floor weeping all night long. The next morning my son got up and saw me laying on the floor and said to me "Mommy I miss you, Mommy I love you." I told him I loved him too, as he was walking back to his room he stopped at the archway, looked over his shoulder and said to me with a sorrow that was incredible for a 3 year old…he said to me "No! I really miss you!" I felt nothing but conviction and said to him "You know what son, I miss me too." This was the beginning of the next chapter of my life. I called my dad and told him I was depressed and needed help. He took me to the hospital, I met with the social worker and they admitted me.

I said all of that to say this, God's love for us is unconditional and it's non-intrusive. He's waiting for us to come to Him and ask for His help. These three words changed my life "Lord, Help Me!" That help came from the words out of the two and a half foot stature of my son.

Who should we pray for?

No matter what we believe about prayer there is

always someone, somewhere saying a prayer for you. Just as we would pray for others we should pray for ourselves. We should pray for our family, our fathers and mothers, our grandfathers and grandmothers, our sisters and brothers, our sons and our daughters. We should include our uncles and aunts, nieces and nephews, cousins and friends, neighbors and enemies. We should pray for the sick, the well, the imprisoned and free. Doctors need prayer, lawyers need prayer, the government needs prayer, the young and old, those living and not yet born. People near and far the list is endless. There is always something or someone we can pray for. So the next time you want to use a set order of words to complain or be critical about something or someone; try praying something positive instead.

Who can you pray for now? I challenge you to make a list of 10 people and/or things that you could pray about:

Prayer List:

1. _____
_____
2. _____
_____
3. _____
_____
4. _____
_____

5. _____
6. _____
7. _____
8. _____
9. _____
10. _____

Prayer:

Lord, thank you for this day and all that you have done for me. Thank you for the opportunity to come to you and ask for your help. As I pray, I ask that you would give me direction and wisdom as I pray for
(insert what you have listed above) regarding

_____
_____
_____
_____

I am also asking that you increase my faith and trust in you as I embark on my journey through prayer. Help me to accept myself authentically and forgive myself for my past mistakes. As I learn to love, forgive and accept myself, teach me to forgive, love and accept others. Help me to accomplish my passion in life and fulfill my current purpose. Help me to have peace with the circumstances I can't change and give me courage to make changes that's needed within myself. Thank you for hearing my prayer. Now open my eyes and ears to see and hear your divine answer.

Important note:

Whatever your passion is make sure to do some work in the direction of fulfilling it. *Faith apart from works is dead*! (James 2:26 ESV)

3

WHEN SHOULD WE PRAY?

We see and hear warning signs everyday all around us. "In case of emergency pull", "Stop", "Emergency Exit Only", "For Emergencies Call 911." For the most part we don't give these instructions a second thought unless we are faced with a catastrophe.

Sadly to say this is how a lot of people view prayer. In case of emergency and before meals. Although these are good times to pray, God intended for prayer to be far more frequent than just during times of crisis or before meals. God wants to hear about celebratory events, tragic events, the good and bad; even mundane. God wants to be included in your everyday life. So no matter how big or small, you can pray about it all at any time.

We must understand that prayer isn't solely for asking for something; it includes being thankful and adoration as well. Think about this…how do you feel when someone you haven't heard from in a while calls you out the blue just to say hello compared to someone who calls only when they need something? As for me, it makes me feel cared for and appreciated. I feel even more special when they think enough of me to share important events taking place in their life. As for the one that calls only in a time of need, those calls are more likely to be ignored. This interaction is predicated on the type of relationship you share with the individual. The difference between us and God is, God will always answer your call and He won't complain. Whether you're just checking in or in need of help.

In order to build any type of relationship, you must not be afraid to communicate openly and honestly. God is always ready to hear from you. So no matter what's going on in your life God has an open ear waiting to listen.

Don't get things misconstrued, just as God is listening, He is also speaking. You must be willing to listen as well. Communication is an exchange that goes two ways. Someone talks the other listens, comprehend and then reply. The cycle continues until it resolves.

We pray all the time and not realize that we're actually praying. It is subconsciously done. We send subliminal petitions all day every day. Just think about it. From the moment you wake until the moment you wake again your mind is transmitting or processing information. No matter how simple or complex your mind is constantly sending and receiving both spiritual and sensual messages. The construction of the human soul is spiritual and prayer is spiritual communication.

It's important for us not to take life for granted. We should be thankful for and in all things. It's unfortunate that it takes us to be faced with the threat of losing something or someone in order for us to appreciate the gift it has been to us.

I remember when I was a young girl, my grandmother; my father's mother went to bed able to see and woke up blind the next morning. The same thing happened to my mother's father. Although the events were years apart, both had strokes of the optic nerve which caused their blindness.

My grandmother's last visual memory of me was me being small enough to duck under the kitchen table and play for hours. She made reference of this mostly every time I visited. I remember my grandfather stressing the importance of us taking care of our eyes all the time. Not just seeing an optometrist for eye exams but seeing an ophthalmologist to check the health of our eyes. So I often wondered if he knew he was eventually going to lose his eye sight.

I was extremely fortunate to have my grandparents apart of my life well into my adult years. Although they have all passed on I am grateful for the lesson in being thankful for my eyesight each day. I watched my grandparents lose their ability to drive, walk unassisted outdoors; although my grandmother would walk across the street to our house from time to time; talking about scary! She said she would listen for traffic and slide her feet to feel for sidewalks, grass and curbs. This woman would even cook; house full of smoke! OMG...talking about terrifying! Walking into the house, I thought it was on fire. As I walked into the kitchen shaken and amazed grandma was cooking grandpa's breakfast about to die from smoke inhalation. Grandpa loved burnt bacon and she was burning it! Grandpa was in the basement and she was trying to help by cooking this particular day. This lady was determined to defy the odds, even if it meant burning the house down...LOL! Talking about when to pray that was definitely a time to. I'm glad my prayer was answered. No one was hurt, grandpa had his burnt bacon and the house was still standing. Needless to say, grandma was forbidden to touch the stove from that day on.

These events might seem extreme but my grandparents losing certain abilities didn't stop them from praying daily. I witnessed them on several occasions and even secretly prayed with them as they were praying and heard them say my name while praying. So if I ever doubted that someone was praying for me, I heard firsthand who was.

We should pray consciously daily. It doesn't matter what you're praying about, just take some time every day and pray. It can be in the morning when you wake. At least say thank you for another day and if you can see be thankful for your eye sight. If you can move be thankful for limb activity and if you can relieve yourself be thankful for natural bodily functions. God forbid you experience loss of any of these abilities, don't take them for granted be thankful. It doesn't take much time to say thank you and the morning time is a good time to say it.

You can pray before leaving the house. Ask for protection from seen and unseen dangers. Your desire is to make it to your destination safely without any incidents. Just ask God to watch over you and those who are out with and around you. We should consciously cover others in our prayers. Be intentional when you pray. Prayer isn't about how many words you can pray a minute, it's about being sincere and specific not ambiguous. If you're unsure of the details or have trouble articulating you thoughts, be broad. God hears the thoughts and intents of your heart. For instance, if you're saying a prayer of thanksgiving just say "Thank you". What are you saying thank you for? In a broad sense you could be thankful for all things pertaining to life. You can ask God to allow you to make to through the day by mere asking God keep me safe. The list is endless. The goal here is simple; to get you to consciously pray.

Night time is as good as any other time to pray. At the end of your day you can reconcile all the events that transpired and you'll see it's a good time to be thankful. You made it through morning traffic; you made it to and from work, with minimal incidents during evening rush hour and everything in between. And for those whose day is just beginning at night technically it's your morning. That's something to be thankful for.

During a crisis it's impractical for one to think that the

first thing on one's mind is to consciously pray. Most are panic stricken and it usually takes someone that isn't emotionally attached or irrational to remind us or lead us in prayer.

When you pray during a crisis, it provides a sense of hope and peace knowing that you're not facing things alone. When confronted with some of life's most uncomfortable circumstances, prayer is a place of solace. Through prayer you can gather your thoughts, acknowledge your feelings, seek direction, and focus your attention specifically on what is going on and the desired outcome.

During times of crisis this isn't the time to lose heart; this is when your faith is needed the most. You will find just how courageous you are when you face the fear of the unknown. Don't expend time playing out all sorts of what if scenarios in your mind. If it hasn't happened don't focus your attention on any negative outcome. Deal with things as they occur. The mind is a conceptual entity always proliferating. It's like an unruly and untrained child needing guidance. If your destructive thought patterns are allowed to linger they will create a living hell for you. Be assured of this one thing, no matter how difficult things may seem the human spirit is resilient and is able to overcome any obstacle.

Pray when you're happy, when you're sad, during good times and bad; any time throughout your day is the perfect time for you to pray.

4
WHERE SHOULD WE PRAY?

Picture these two scenarios. 1.) It's Sunday morning, you're at church and it's prayer time. As you stand at the altar, the individual that was chosen to lead prayer begins praying ostentatiously using all sorts of theatrics and elaborate words; boasting and bragging. It seemed they had rehearsed all week long just for this special presentation, which was more like a message to the congregants rather than a prayer to God. 2.) While walking at the park you witness a religious group praying loudly, judging and condemning people to hell; making a public spectacle of themselves.

In the first scenario prayer was taking place indoors.

As for the second, prayer was taking place outdoors. Where was the proper place to pray? Indoors or outdoors? The truth of the matter is, "It doesn't matter." The issue isn't the physical location of your being but rather the furtive places of your heart while you are praying. Are you praying from a place of truth and humility? Or are you praying from a place of haughtiness and hypocrisy?

In these two scenarios these individuals are mirrored reflections of the Pharisees in the bible. The Pharisees were known for making public spectacles of themselves. They were braggadocios and would demean and diminish others. They were full of hypocrisy and pride. They lacked sincerity of heart. I'm sure you know or know someone who knows someone of this nature. This is not the way you should pray. Check the place of your heart.

Prayer should be viewed as a private and an intimate practice. Sacred! You need to protect your place of prayer. When you are consciously praying, only those that you would entrust your soul with should partake in prayer with you if you are inviting others to pray along. You must be selective, use your intuition when allowing people to pray for and with you. Trust your gut feeling. Don't ignore it. Prayer is essential and should not be taken lightly.

Some would say there are conflicting messages when it comes to where we should pray; should we pray in public or not? In the book of Matthew, Jesus stated *"But when you pray, go into your room and shut the door and pray to your Father who is in secret. And your Father who sees in secret will reward you.*"(Matthew 6:6 ESV) Now if we analyze when Jesus prayed for an extended period of time we will find the places Jesus prayed according to the bible were outdoors. In Matthew 14:23, he went up into a mountain…alone; and in Matthew 26:36, he went to a place called Gethsemane and prayed alone. Although his disciples were there with him, he left from among them and went off to pray alone. In the book of Mark, he went into a deserted place and in Luke he went to the wilderness. Not only was he outdoors, he prayed alone with the exception of when he took three of the twelve disciples with him to pray on a mountain.

So what did Jesus mean when he said "go into your room and shut the door?" Was he speaking figuratively or literally? It is my belief he was speaking figuratively. One thing was evident when Jesus prayed, he left from among his followers to be alone. So to go into your room and shut the door means go alone to a private place and pray. If he meant this literally then his actions were hypocritical.

Because prayer is private and mainly takes place alone, you can secretly pray anywhere, not only in synagogues, temples, chapels or mosques. There aren't any "No Prayer Zones" that prohibit prayer. So you're safe to pray anywhere as long as you're not making a spectacle of yourself.

During my hospitalization, I remember the elevator doors opening and two people standing there waiting for me to enter onto the floor. The young lady said "Hi! We've been waiting for you." The last thing I wanted was to be bothered by anyone. She grabbed me by the hand, walked me over to a bench where we sat. She seemed to be really happy to see me. She introduced the gentleman as Pastor Bruce and then asked my name. I hung my head and said in a weak voice "Kim." She forcefully said "NO! Listen to me. Look at me!" She said with such confidence and conviction "Hi! My name is Carlotta, what's yours?" I replied again unconvincingly "My name is Kimberly." She urged me again to look at her but this time requesting me to sit up straight. She introduced herself once more "My name is Carlotta, what's yours?" I sat up straight, took in a deep breath and belted out "My name is Kimberly Maddox." She smiled and said "If you don't like your name you are rejecting yourself. Accepting yourself begins with knowing your name." She charged me with the assignment of praying for everyone who asked for prayer while she and Bruce committed to pray for me. This was inconceivable to me, especially when I felt inadequate and in need of prayer myself. To make a long story short, I committed to my assignment and even when I didn't want to I prayed; and prayed, and prayed. I watched the prayers be answered. I saw patients getting well and being discharged. I prayed and they prayed until it was time for my discharge. Little did I know, as I was praying for others I was being strengthened and healed myself. Praying became my new normal, my assigned place!

As you see, hospitals are a great place to pray; whether you're the patient or you're praying for a patient. Another place people find themselves praying is the workplace. Many people pray at work; especially during long boring meetings. A prayer during that time would probably go something like this, "Oh God, please let this meeting hurry up and end." And as soon as they announce the meeting is over, the first words that probably comes to mind are…"Amen" or "Thank you God!"

We pray in our cars. We pray on planes. We pray at school, on buses and trains. There are countless places we can pray. At the park while walking the dog, at the gym while taking a jog, in the shower, just take a minute; no place is off limits.

Whenever you feel the desire to pray, find your quiet space. It doesn't matter the physical location, more importantly make sure to go with a pure and sincere of heart.

List 5 places you could go to pray. Make a commitment to go there and pray. Write down the place, date and what you prayed.

Place_____ Date_____

Prayer:_____
_____
_____
_____
_____
_____
_____
_____
_____

Place_____ Date_____

Prayer:_____
_____
_____
_____
_____
_____
_____
_____
_____
_____
_____
_____

Place_____ Date_____

Prayer:_____
_____
_____
_____
_____
_____
_____
_____
_____
_____
_____
_____

PRECARIUS

Place_____ Date_____

Prayer:_____
_____
_____
_____
_____
_____
_____
_____
_____
_____
_____
_____
_____

Place_____ Date_____

Prayer:_____
_____
_____
_____
_____
_____
_____
_____
_____
_____
_____
_____
_____

5
WHY SHOULD WE PRAY?

There are many reasons why people choose not to pray; some of those reasons may include: unbelief, guilt, disappointment, rejection, fear or feelings of unworthiness. Being confounded by what is perceived as an unanswered prayer can leave you disheartened, discontented and questioning why.

Life is filled with "why" questions. Why do bad things happen to good people? Why is there so much suffering in the world? Why hasn't my prayers been answered? These questions may never be answered to our liking. Although objectionable nonetheless they are answered.

At the heart of these questions is our relationship with

God. Let's face it, when bad things happen God is the first one we question or place blame. The fact is, some questions in life the answers we'll never understand and we need to accept that. There are circumstances in life that are not within the realm of our control. Understandably, things happen; it's all a part of the cycle of life.

When we encounter spiritual obstacles and quandaries the answer to the question "Why should we pray?" is a simple one. Although there are many reasons why one should pray, the principal reason is that prayer connects us to the heart of God. Prayer is the essential source in cultivating a fruitful relationship with God and understanding the definition of our life's purposes and His plan. Through prayer we receive guidance and wisdom. It can produce tangible evidence in what is sometimes seen as impossible or irreversible circumstances; thus impacting the human experience and directly affecting the course of life. Prayer is the bridge to knowing our authentic selves and the God who created us.

Within each of us there is a longing for meaningful connection. One of our deepest needs as humans is to feel connected through relationships. Prayer is the means by which we connect with the Divine. In order to foster a meaningful relationship with God we must pray.

Other reasons why we should pray: Prayer helps us to cope with life's challenges, frustrations and fears. Praying and keeping vigil shows compassion and support for those that are hurting during trying times. We offer prays of thanksgiving during auspicious occasions; such as the birth of a baby, weddings, graduations, birthdays, anniversaries and more. We pray to ask God's blessing for all we aspire to do.

Prayer helps you to open up and listen from within. Prayer aids us in discovering who we are authentically and what our passion in life is. Prayer provides clarity and guidance as you live through your life.

You must be vulnerable in prayer, not protective or guarded. You must patiently persevere, waiting for the answers you are courageously seeking.

Some people pray for worldly benefits; while other for spiritual growth. No matter the reason you pray, God is willing to hear them all. Be open-minded, because with prayer you don't get to choose the outcome. But what you do get to choose is your response or reaction to the outcome. Keep in mind there is always a bigger picture, a greater plan than what you may see. Things aren't always exactly how you see them. Vision is perceptive. You must be willing to see things from different perspectives. Not just from where you are. Know that there is a purpose working within everything as long as we subsist.

> *"in Order to form a more perfect Union, establish Justice, insure domestic Tranquility, provide for the common defense, promote the general Welfare, and secure the Blessings of Liberty to ourselves and our Posterity,"* (Preamble U.S. Constitution)
> We must pray!

Identify some obstacles that may be preventing you from praying. Perhaps people? Your past? In life there are some circumstances that are beyond our control. Unfortunately people and our past are among them. However we do possess the ability within us to change our thoughts and feelings, which will ultimately impact our outcomes.

Consider your feelings. Write them down in the space provided below. For instance: fear, guilt, shame, anger, etc. Acknowledge their existence and acknowledge their origin and how they came to be. In other words, what happened that caused this effect? Validate it by saying something like "I had the right to feel _____ because _____ happened. I no longer have to feel _____ because _____ is no longer happening." Know that you are safe, you are loved, and you are forgiven. Look in the mirror and say to yourself audibly, "I forgive you." and "I love you." Show yourself kindness, patience and understanding just like you would show your best friend who was experiencing a dilemma. And if those feelings try to arrest you again, don't ignore them. Acknowledge them and remind yourself they have been forgiven and they no longer have the right to hold you captive. I pray, may you be free from all of your past, current and future uncontrollable circumstances and may you will live in the liberty of your today.

PRECARIUS

List Obstacles - Past, Present and Potential:

6

HOW SHOULD WE PRAY?

Prayer is tailored to the individual. There is not a particular posture or vernacular you must absolutely use in order to pray. There is no magic involved. Theatrics, lip service and temperamental outbursts are vain. Prayer isn't role play. We don't have to dress, look or speak according to religious standards or the traditions of men. God is not impressed with titles or social standing. You don't have to be of a certain age, ethnicity, gender or religion. Prayer is for us all.

When you pray, pray with sincerity and transparency; hope, conviction and humility. Be sure and specific. Before rushing into making requests, acknowledge and reverence God for who He is; the Creator and Sustainer of all things. Show gratitude for all He has already done for you. Know that God knows what is best for you and will answer you according to where you are in your life and in His timing.

Pray with confidence. Confidence in knowing that with God all things are possible; anything can happen. Take note of the words "all" and "anything". These words are all encompassing and should be treated as such. Not just what we perceive as good but that which is perceived as bad as well. Remember perception is not total reality it's not the absolute truth. So as you pray be aware that you are a part of a greater plan.

Know that you can take all your cares and concerns to God in prayer. When it seems like answers have been deferred, your confidence may be challenged but don't give up. This is when you need to be persistent and patient. Ask for clarity of thought, guidance and assistance when you feel the need to give way to fears, concerns or anxieties. Ask for healing and transmutation; healing from your negative thought patterns and past disappointments. Transmutation simply means to change into another form. Ask God to change your fear to faith, your concern to contentment and your anxiety to peace. Trust that you are loved and supported. You are not alone. Know that all is going according to Divine plan.

Prayer is personal and private. It is not to be taken lightly and shared with everyone. Prayer is sacred and should be secret; between you and God. You don't need mediation from anyone in order to make your petition. If you have the desire for someone to join you in prayer make sure that individual is sincere and trustworthy. Unfortunately you can't trust everyone with something so precious. Pray for discernment and ask God to show you who you can invite into your intimate circumference with Him.

When you put your trust in someone, that usually means they have something you feel you need. They are filling a need. The problem with this is that we are putting trust in fickle man. Trusting and relying on their finite abilities, crafty words and empty promises. People have the tendency to let you down and betray your trust. That's why it's important not to put your confidence in people, it is better to put your trust in God.

God is Truth. Truth is Eternal, perpetual and unchanging. Truth is superior to any problem or circumstance. The truth is God believes in you. Situations and trials are God's testimonies to us. So take heart and thank God for all things that come. Problems come to test our faith and strengthen our resolve. We must be fully aware of our strengths and weaknesses if we are going to be able to foster full productive prayer lives.

In your own words how should you pray?

_____
_____
_____
_____

7

PRAYERS OF DAVID

We're going to examine two prayers King David prayed in the book of Psalms. These prayers show the imperfection of this King; prone to mistakes, regrets, frustrations and shame. David had an intensely passionate love for God and sincere heart toward him.; although he committed some of the most reprehensible sins recorded in the Old Testament. David was the head of an extremely dysfunctional family. He was an adulterer, murderer and polygamist. He is also known for his elaborate skills as a warrior and a writer of many psalms. David's life was waves of extreme emotions. We can learn immensely from David and his relationship with God as well as empathize with some of his struggles.

Psalms 139
(ESV Bible)

1 O Lord, you have searched me and known me! 2 You know when I sit down and when I rise up; you discern my thoughts from afar. 3 You search out my path and my lying down and are acquainted with all my ways. 4 Even before a word is on my tongue, behold, O Lord, you know it altogether. 5 You hem me in, behind and before, and lay your hand upon me. 6 Such knowledge is too wonderful for me; it is high; I cannot attain it. 7 Where shall I go from your Spirit? Or where shall I flee from your presence? 8 If I ascend to heaven, you are there! If I make my bed in Sheol, you are there! 9 If I take the wings of the morning and dwell in the uttermost parts of the sea, 10 even there your hand shall lead me, and your right hand shall hold me. 11 If I say, "Surely the darkness shall cover me, and the light about me be night," 12 even the darkness is not dark to you; the night is bright as the day, for darkness is as light with you. 13 For you formed my inward parts; you knitted me together in my mother's womb. 14 I praise you, for I am fearfully and wonderfully made. Wonderful are your works; my soul knows it very well. 15 My frame was not hidden from you, when I was being made in secret, intricately woven in the depths of the earth. 16 Your eyes saw my unformed substance; in your book were written, every one of them, the days that were formed for me, when as yet there was none of them. 17 How precious to me are your thoughts, O God! How vast is the sum of them! 18 If I would count them, they are more than the sand. I awake, and I am still with you. 19 Oh that you would slay the wicked, O God! O men of blood, depart from me! 20 They speak against you with malicious intent; your enemies take your name in vain. 21 Do I not hate those who hate you, O Lord? And do I not loathe those who rise up against you? 22 I hate them with complete hatred; I count them my enemies. 23 Search me, O God, and know my heart! Try me and know my thoughts! 24 And see if there be any grievous way in me, and lead me in the way everlasting!

What does Psalms 139 mean?

This Psalm is in 4 parts:

- ❖ Verses 1-6. God knows all about us.

- ❖ Verses 7-12. We cannot hide from God.

- ❖ Verses 13-18. God created (made) us.

- ❖ Verses 19-24. David prays about his enemies and himself.

Verses 1-6

There is nothing about us God doesn't know. So you might be asking, "If God already knows everything about us what is the use of praying?" Remember praying isn't about what God knows about us; it's about building a relationship with Him and getting to know Him.

There are people in your life that know things about your character because of your relationship with them.

Yet and still they may ask you to explain your behavior. You know at times they can detect when you're lying and when you're telling the truth. Despite this knowledge, fear of rejection doesn't stop you from fostering a closer relationship with them. This truth may even cause you to feel closer because they accept you as you are. Contrary to what some believe, God accepts you faults and all.

Verses 7-12

There is no place we can run to there is no where we can hide from the presence of God. No place in heaven, neither on earth, sea nor in hell. In your darkest place, God is your guiding light. God is everywhere you go. He's able to be everywhere with you because He lives in you. You can't escape Him. He created us as His habitation. It could be a conceivably awkward position to live with someone who never speaks to you and yet say they love you. Often times this is what our relationship looks like with God; living together but no interaction or communication. Prayer is simply communicating from your heart to God.

Verses 13-18

God meticulously fashioned you in the secret place of your mother's womb. There is nothing bad about you; it's all good! You should praise God for how He intricately put you together. Don't mistake this shaping as moral shaping. We are taught morals. This shaping was spiritual and physical. God didn't make a mistake when He created you as you are. Again, He didn't create your moral fiber don't confuse this. Moral character is developed by the environment in which we dwell. We learn what is acceptable from our homes, schools, churches, and the people in which we surround ourselves. God created your spiritual fiber and chose you to be physically male or female.

All of your days have been predetermined; the pathways of your life. God's thoughts toward you are infinite; greater than your mind can conceive. Thoughts that are good not evil; day and night God is thoughtful of you.

Verses 19-24

There is a swift change in the next four verses. David prayed a pray of imprecation for his enemies. He called them wicked and murderous men. David loved God so much that he loathed those that abhorred God. He counted God's enemies as his own and wanted God to slay them. David knew God knew all his thoughts but his ultimate desire was to please God so he asked God to search his heart and mind for any grievous ways and lead him to the right way which is truth and everlasting.

Psalms 51
(ESV Bible)

__1__ Have mercy on me, O God, according to your steadfast love; according to your abundant mercy blot out my transgressions. __2__ Wash me thoroughly from my iniquity, and cleanse me from my sin! __3__ For I know my transgressions, and my sin is ever before me. __4__ Against you, you only, have I sinned and done what is evil in your sight, so that you may be justified in your words and blameless in your judgment. __5__ Behold, I was brought forth in iniquity, and in sin did my mother conceive me. __6__ Behold, you delight in truth in the inward being, and you teach me wisdom in the secret heart. __7__ Purge me with hyssop, and I shall be clean; wash me, and I shall be whiter than snow. __8__ Let me hear joy and gladness; let the bones that you have broken rejoice. __9__ Hide your face from my sins, and blot out all my iniquities. __10__ Create in me a clean heart, O God, and renew a right spirit within me. __11__ Cast me not away from your presence, and take not your Holy Spirit from me. __12__ Restore to me the joy of your salvation, and uphold me with a willing spirit. __13__ Then I will teach transgressors your ways, and sinners will return to you. __14__ Deliver me from blood guiltiness, O God, O God of my salvation, and my tongue will sing aloud of your righteousness. __15__ O Lord, open my lips, and my mouth will declare your praise. __16__ For you will not delight in sacrifice, or I would give it; you will not be pleased with a burnt offering. __17__ The sacrifices of God are a broken spirit; a broken and contrite heart, O God, you will not despise. __18__ Do good to Zion in your good pleasure; build up the walls of Jerusalem; __19__ then will you delight in right sacrifices, in burnt offerings and whole burnt offerings; then bulls will be offered on your altar.

David's Repentance

This prayer David prayed after he allowed one night of lust with the wife of Uriah, Bathsheba caused dire consequences in his life. David was a great warrior but he couldn't overcome the war within himself. We are all one decision away from wreaking havoc or bringing bliss into our lives. There is a battle going on within each and every one of us; our own secret mission to overcome what seems to be insurmountable obstacles. We can be overcomers but we need God's help.

David knew that no matter what he could rely on God. David was courageous enough to put his trust in God. For he knew God was trustworthy. In spite of his immoral actions David didn't allow his embarrassment and pride to keep him from going to God. He knew it was God alone he sinned against and his heart was fractured as broken glass. He cried out in anguish because of what he had done. His spirit was fractured as broken glass and his conscious was stained with blood.

David entreated for God to have mercy on him and to forget his debauchery. He asked God to wash away the guilt that comes with doing the wrong things. David recalls his sin, it has forever been seared in his mind.

David didn't want to be the way he was, so he asked God to create him a clean heart and renew His Divine spirit within him. David heavily depended on the presence of God to be with him and dreaded the thought of losing it. He was in agony and lost all hope and joy. He desired to be restored and would show his gratitude by teaching and proclaiming to others.

David understood these fundamental things; God sees the spirit of you and knows the intentions of your heart. He knows when you are truly repentant. God will not despise a broken spirit, a broken and contrite heart.

No matter the level of wrong you have done, God will not reject you if you come to Him with a broken spirit, a broken and contrite heart asking for His forgiveness.

Life Lessons We Can Learn From David

- ❖ Self-examination is essential to recognizing our own sin, and then we must truly repent. We might fool ourselves and others at times, but there is no hiding from God.

- ❖ God always offers forgiveness, but we can't escape the consequences of our actions. With every decision there are consequences, be it positive or negative.

- ❖ God values our faith in Him. In spite of life's ups and downs, He is always there to comfort and guide us. All we need to do is ask.

Answer the following questions:

PRECARIUS

What is prayer?

Who should pray and to whom?

When should you pray?

Where should you pray?

Why should you pray?

How should you pray?

In what ways does David's life reflect yours?

What can you do to build a closer relationship with God?

8
PRAYER JOURNALING

There are several ways to commune with God. One way I find extremely effective is through prayer journaling. You'll be amazed how God answers your prayers and keeping a journal allows you to record the experience.

Pay close attention to what you pray so you can recognize when an answer is manifest. There are numerous ways God can send you an answer. Your answer could come in a message from a friend or stranger. It could come through any form of media or publication. Answers are found in nature including within you.

I invite you to take the 36.5 prayer challenge. All you have to do is make a vow to pray 36.5 days within one year for at least 24 minutes a day. You choose the days and allot your time. Journal every prayer and as you receive answers record them as well. Make sure to include the date and time of your prayers and answers.

My prayer for you is that you will begin to build an unshakeable relationship with God; knowing that He is concerned and cares for you. I also pray that as you pray your heart be open and fertile and the garden of your mind be cultivated. I pray your ears will hear and receive divine direction and your eyes to see beyond your natural perception. I pray that you pray with a sincere heart and take hold of the good in all things, no matter how grim. May God bless you on this journey as you define your relationship with Him through prayer.

Alone you cry thousands of tears until you're totally numb
You might appear to be overwhelmed with pride smiling from ear to ear
Although you laugh until it cramps your side and takes your breath away
Stop denying and continuously hiding all you're going through
There's help, there's hope, call out to God
He's waiting to hear from you.

*"Be Encouraged, Be Blessed, Be Enriched,
most of all Be Authentically You!"*

Kimberly E.M. Beasley

36.5 DAYS OF PRAYER

DAY 1

Date_____ Time_____

Prayer_____
_____
_____
_____
_____
_____
_____
_____
_____
_____
_____
_____
_____
_____

Date_____ Time_____

Answer_____
_____
_____
_____
_____
_____
_____
_____
_____
_____
_____

DAY 2

Date_____ Time_____

Prayer_____
_____
_____
_____
_____
_____
_____
_____
_____
_____
_____
_____
_____
_____
_____

Date_____ Time_____

Answer_____
_____
_____
_____
_____
_____
_____
_____
_____
_____
_____

DAY 3

Date_____ Time_____

Prayer_____
_____
_____
_____
_____
_____
_____
_____
_____
_____
_____
_____
_____
_____
_____
_____

Date_____ Time_____

Answer_____
_____
_____
_____
_____
_____
_____
_____
_____
_____
_____
_____

DAY 4

Date_____ Time_____

Prayer_____
_____
_____
_____
_____
_____
_____
_____
_____
_____
_____
_____
_____
_____
_____

Date_____ Time_____

Answer_____
_____
_____
_____
_____
_____
_____
_____
_____
_____
_____

DAY 5

Date_____ Time_____

Prayer_____
_____
_____
_____
_____
_____
_____
_____
_____
_____
_____
_____
_____
_____
_____

Date_____ Time_____

Answer_____
_____
_____
_____
_____
_____
_____
_____
_____
_____
_____
_____

DAY 6

Date_____ Time_____

Prayer_____
_____
_____
_____
_____
_____
_____
_____
_____
_____
_____
_____
_____
_____
_____

Date_____ Time_____

Answer_____
_____
_____
_____
_____
_____
_____
_____
_____
_____
_____
_____

DAY 7

Date_____ Time_____

Prayer_____
_____
_____
_____
_____
_____
_____
_____
_____
_____
_____
_____
_____
_____
_____

Date_____ Time_____

Answer_____
_____
_____
_____
_____
_____
_____
_____
_____
_____
_____

DAY 8

Date_____ Time_____

Prayer_____
_____
_____
_____
_____
_____
_____
_____
_____
_____
_____
_____
_____
_____
_____

Date_____ Time_____

Answer_____
_____
_____
_____
_____
_____
_____
_____
_____
_____
_____

DAY 9

Date_____ Time_____

Prayer_____
_____
_____
_____
_____
_____
_____
_____
_____
_____
_____
_____
_____
_____
_____
_____

Date_____ Time_____

Answer_____
_____
_____
_____
_____
_____
_____
_____
_____
_____
_____
_____

DAY 10

Date_____ Time_____

Prayer_____
_____
_____
_____
_____
_____
_____
_____
_____
_____
_____
_____
_____
_____
_____

Date_____ Time_____

Answer_____
_____
_____
_____
_____
_____
_____
_____
_____
_____
_____

DAY 11

Date_____ Time_____

Prayer_____
_____
_____
_____
_____
_____
_____
_____
_____
_____
_____
_____
_____
_____
_____

Date_____ Time_____

Answer_____
_____
_____
_____
_____
_____
_____
_____
_____
_____
_____

DAY 12

Date_____ Time_____

Prayer_____
_____
_____
_____
_____
_____
_____
_____
_____
_____
_____
_____
_____
_____
_____
_____

Date_____ Time_____

Answer_____
_____
_____
_____
_____
_____
_____
_____
_____
_____
_____
_____

DAY 13

Date_____ Time_____

Prayer_____
_____
_____
_____
_____
_____
_____
_____
_____
_____
_____
_____
_____
_____
_____

Date_____ Time_____

Answer_____
_____
_____
_____
_____
_____
_____
_____
_____
_____
_____

DAY 14

Date_____ Time_____

Prayer_____
_____
_____
_____
_____
_____
_____
_____
_____
_____
_____
_____
_____
_____

Date_____ Time_____

Answer_____
_____
_____
_____
_____
_____
_____
_____
_____
_____
_____
_____

DAY 15

Date_____ Time_____

Prayer_____
_____
_____
_____
_____
_____
_____
_____
_____
_____
_____
_____
_____
_____
_____
_____

Date_____ Time_____

Answer_____
_____
_____
_____
_____
_____
_____
_____
_____
_____
_____
_____

DAY 16

Date_____ Time_____

Prayer_____
_____
_____
_____
_____
_____
_____
_____
_____
_____
_____
_____
_____
_____
_____

Date_____ Time_____

Answer_____
_____
_____
_____
_____
_____
_____
_____
_____
_____
_____
_____

DAY 17

Date_____ Time_____

Prayer_____
_____
_____
_____
_____
_____
_____
_____
_____
_____
_____
_____
_____
_____

Date_____ Time_____

Answer_____
_____
_____
_____
_____
_____
_____
_____
_____
_____

DAY 18

Date_____ Time_____

Prayer_____
_____
_____
_____
_____
_____
_____
_____
_____
_____
_____
_____
_____
_____

Date_____ Time_____

Answer_____
_____
_____
_____
_____
_____
_____
_____
_____
_____
_____

DAY 19

Date_____ Time_____

Prayer_____
_____
_____
_____
_____
_____
_____
_____
_____
_____
_____
_____
_____
_____
_____
_____

Date_____ Time_____

Answer_____
_____
_____
_____
_____
_____
_____
_____
_____
_____
_____
_____

DAY 20

Date_____ Time_____

Prayer_____
_____
_____
_____
_____
_____
_____
_____
_____
_____
_____
_____
_____
_____

Date_____ Time_____

Answer_____
_____
_____
_____
_____
_____
_____
_____
_____
_____
_____

DAY 21

Date_____ Time_____

Prayer_____
_____
_____
_____
_____
_____
_____
_____
_____
_____
_____
_____
_____
_____
_____

Date_____ Time_____

Answer_____
_____
_____
_____
_____
_____
_____
_____
_____
_____
_____

DAY 22

Date_____ Time_____

Prayer_____
_____
_____
_____
_____
_____
_____
_____
_____
_____
_____
_____
_____
_____

Date_____ Time_____

Answer_____
_____
_____
_____
_____
_____
_____
_____
_____
_____
_____

DAY 23

Date_____ Time_____

Prayer_____
_____
_____
_____
_____
_____
_____
_____
_____
_____
_____
_____
_____
_____
_____

Date_____ Time_____

Answer_____
_____
_____
_____
_____
_____
_____
_____
_____
_____
_____

DAY 24

Date_____ Time_____

Prayer_____
_____
_____
_____
_____
_____
_____
_____
_____
_____
_____
_____
_____
_____
_____

Date_____ Time_____

Answer_____
_____
_____
_____
_____
_____
_____
_____
_____
_____
_____
_____

DAY 25

Date_____ Time_____

Prayer_____
_____
_____
_____
_____
_____
_____
_____
_____
_____
_____
_____
_____
_____
_____

Date_____ Time_____

Answer_____
_____
_____
_____
_____
_____
_____
_____
_____
_____
_____

DAY 26

Date_____ Time_____

Prayer_____
_____
_____
_____
_____
_____
_____
_____
_____
_____
_____
_____
_____
_____
_____

Date_____ Time_____

Answer_____
_____
_____
_____
_____
_____
_____
_____
_____
_____
_____
_____

DAY 27

Date_____ Time_____

Prayer_____
_____
_____
_____
_____
_____
_____
_____
_____
_____
_____
_____
_____
_____
_____

Date_____ Time_____

Answer_____
_____
_____
_____
_____
_____
_____
_____
_____
_____
_____
_____
_____

DAY 28

Date_____ Time_____

Prayer_____
_____
_____
_____
_____
_____
_____
_____
_____
_____
_____
_____
_____
_____
_____

Date_____ Time_____

Answer_____
_____
_____
_____
_____
_____
_____
_____
_____
_____
_____
_____
_____

DAY 29

Date_____ Time_____

Prayer_____
_____
_____
_____
_____
_____
_____
_____
_____
_____
_____
_____
_____
_____

Date_____ Time_____

Answer_____
_____
_____
_____
_____
_____
_____
_____
_____
_____
_____

DAY 30

Date_____ Time_____

Prayer_____
_____
_____
_____
_____
_____
_____
_____
_____
_____
_____
_____
_____
_____
_____

Date_____ Time_____

Answer_____
_____
_____
_____
_____
_____
_____
_____
_____
_____
_____
_____

DAY 31

Date_____ Time_____

Prayer_____
_____
_____
_____
_____
_____
_____
_____
_____
_____
_____
_____
_____
_____
_____

Date_____ Time_____

Answer_____
_____
_____
_____
_____
_____
_____
_____
_____
_____
_____
_____

DAY 32

Date_____ Time_____

Prayer_____
_____
_____
_____
_____
_____
_____
_____
_____
_____
_____
_____
_____
_____
_____

Date_____ Time_____

Answer_____
_____
_____
_____
_____
_____
_____
_____
_____
_____
_____

DAY 33

Date_____ Time_____

Prayer_____
_____
_____
_____
_____
_____
_____
_____
_____
_____
_____
_____
_____
_____
_____

Date_____ Time_____

Answer_____
_____
_____
_____
_____
_____
_____
_____
_____
_____
_____
_____

DAY 34

Date_____ Time_____

Prayer_____
_____
_____
_____
_____
_____
_____
_____
_____
_____
_____
_____
_____
_____

Date_____ Time_____

Answer_____
_____
_____
_____
_____
_____
_____
_____
_____
_____

PRECARIUS

DAY 35

Date_____ Time_____

Prayer_____
_____
_____
_____
_____
_____
_____
_____
_____
_____
_____
_____
_____
_____
_____

Date_____ Time_____

Answer_____
_____
_____
_____
_____
_____
_____
_____
_____
_____
_____

DAY 36

Date_____ Time_____

Prayer_____
_____
_____
_____
_____
_____
_____
_____
_____
_____
_____
_____
_____
_____
_____

Date_____ Time_____

Answer_____
_____
_____
_____
_____
_____
_____
_____
_____
_____
_____

DAY 36.5

Date_____ Time_____

Prayer_____
_____
_____
_____
_____
_____
_____
_____
_____
_____
_____
_____
_____
_____
_____

Date_____ Time_____

Answer_____
_____
_____
_____
_____
_____
_____
_____
_____
_____
_____
_____

ABOUT THE AUTHOR

Kimberly Elizabeth Maddox-Beasley award winning author, a native of Detroit, Michigan is the youngest of four siblings. She is happily married to the love of her life and best friend. She and her husband share 2 sons. Kimberly and her husband relocated to Texas in 2004 where they currently reside. She attended Texas Woman's University where she majored in Social Work.

In 1998 Kimberly's life was forever changed when she decided to devoted herself to prayer. Kimberly has a profound prayer life and has seen many of her prayers answered. In the face of varied challenges she remained prayerful and is sure that "Prayer" really works.

Kimberly is a gifted Speaker and Spiritual teacher whose mission is to aid individuals in developing a better quality of life by building and strengthening their spirituality and consciousness of God. Her methodology for achieving this is through literary works. Her desire is to see individuals thrive spiritually as well in their personal/familial lives.

Kimberly is a traditional woman with steadfast faith in God. She attributes her overcoming ability to her faith in God, love for herself, coupled with the love and support from her family.

At the core of her beliefs she loves truth, practices justice and pursues righteousness.

Also available from Hunny Child Books and Kimberly E.M. Beasley

Available in paperback and eBook at amazon.com, txauthors.com, barnesandnoble.com, iTunes and more

Revelations Of My Heart
Poems, Prayers, Notes and Quotes
2015 Best Poetry Spiritual Book
Texas Association of Authors

www.hunnychildbooks.com

"Supremacy of God"

www.ingramcontent.com/pod-product-compliance
Lightning Source LLC
Chambersburg PA
CBHW071955070426
42453CB00008BA/798